Plan For Success: How To Plan Your Next Speech

How to plan a speech in order to achieve your goals and delight your audience

"Practical, proven techniques that will help you to make your next speech a success"

Dr. Jim Anderson

Published by:
Blue Elephant Consulting
Tampa, Florida

Copyright © 2014 by Dr. Jim Anderson

All rights reserved. No part of this book may be reproduced of transmitted in any form or by any means, electronic or mechanical, including photocopying, recording or by any information storage and retrieval system without written permission of the publisher, except for inclusion of brief quotations in a review.

Printed in the United States of America

Library of Congress Control Number: 2014918047

ISBN-13: 978-1502745750
ISBN-10: 1502745755

Warning – Disclaimer

The purpose of this book is to educate and entertain. This book does not promise or guarantee that anyone following the ideas, tips, suggestions, techniques or strategies will be hired. It is the discretion of employers if you will or will not be hired. The author, publisher and distributor(s) shall have neither liability nor responsibility to anyone with respect to any loss or damage caused, or alleged to be caused, directly or indirectly by the information contained in this book.

Recent Books By The Author

Product Management

- How Product Managers Can Grow Their Career: How Product Managers Can Find And Succeed In The Right Job

- Product Management Secrets: Techniques For Product Managers To Boost Product Sales And Increase Customer Satisfaction

Public Speaking

- How To Become A Better Speaker By Changing How You Speak: Change techniques that will transform a speech into a memorable event

- How To Give A Great Presentation: Presentation techniques that will transform a speech into a memorable event

CIO Skills

- What CIOs Need To Know About Working With Partners: Techniques For CIOs To Use In Order To Be Able To Successfully Work With Partners

- How CIOs Can Make Innovation Happen: Tips And Techniques For CIOs To Use In Order To Make Innovation Happen In Their IT Department

IT Manager Skills

- How IT Managers Can Make Innovation Happen: Tips And Techniques For IT Managers To Use In Order To Make Innovation Happen In Their Teams

- Secrets Of Effective Leadership For IT Managers: Tips And Techniques That IT Managers Can Use In Order To Develop Leadership Skills

Negotiating

- Learn How To Signal In Your Next Negotiation: How To Develop The Skill Of Effective Signaling In A Negotiation In Order To Get The Best Possible Outcome

- Learn The Skill Of Exploring In A Negotiation: How To Develop The Skill Of Exploring What Is Possible In A Negotiation In Order To Reach The Best Possible Deal

Miscellaneous

- The Internet-Enabled Successful School District Superintendent: How To Use The Internet To Boost Parental Involvement In Your Schools

- Power Distribution Unit (PDU) Secrets: What Everyone Who Works In A Data Center Needs To Know!

Note: See a complete list of books by Dr. Jim Anderson at the back of this book.

Acknowledgements

Any book like this one is the result of years of real-world work experience. In my over 25 years of working for 7 different firms, I have met countless fantastic people and I've been mentored by some truly exceptional ones. Although I've probably forgotten some of the people who made me the person that I am today, here is my attempt to finally give them the recognition that they so truly deserve:

- Thomas P. Anderson
- Art Puett
- Bobbi Marshall
- Bob Boggs

Dr. **Jim** Anderson

This book is dedicated to my family: Lori, Maddie, Nick, and Ben. None of this would have been possible without their constant love and support.

Thanks for always believing in me and providing me with the strength to always be willing to go out there and be my best for you.

Table of Contents

PLAN FOR SUCCESS: HOW TO PLAN YOUR NEXT SPEECH 8

ABOUT THE AUTHOR 10

CHAPTER 1: SPEAKER: YOU ARE WHAT YOU WEAR! 15

CHAPTER 2: HOW TO RIG A SPEECH TO GET THE OUTCOME YOU WANT EVERY TIME 20

CHAPTER 3: BUSINESS SPEAKING IS UNLIKE ANY OTHER SPEAKING .24

CHAPTER 4: GOOD SPEAKERS KNOW HOW TO WORK A ROOM 27

CHAPTER 5: WHY EVERY PUBLIC SPEAKER SHOULD BE "TWEETING" (THIS MEANS YOU) 31

CHAPTER 6: THE ULTIMATE PUBLIC SPEAKING QUESTION: WHAT TO SPEAK ABOUT? 35

CHAPTER 7: PUBLIC SPEAKERS WANT TO KNOW: ARE HANDOUTS YOUR FRIEND OR FOE? 39

CHAPTER 8: BUSINESS SPEAKING: WHAT TO DO, WHAT NOT TO DO 43

CHAPTER 9: BREAK GLASS IN CASE OF SPEECH 47

CHAPTER 10: HOW SPEAKERS SHOULD HANDLE HANDOUTS 50

CHAPTER 11: HEY SPEAKER – WHAT'S YOUR POINT? 54

CHAPTER 12: WAYS TO PLAN AN EFFECTIVE SPEECH 58

Plan For Success:
How To Plan Your Next Speech

As public speakers, the one thing that we all want to be able to learn to do better is to improve how we speak. The key to doing this successfully is to learn how to plan our next speech.

The good news is that planning a speech is actually fairly simple. The first step in making this happen is to understand that the clothes that you wear when you speak will tell your audience a story.

In order to make sure that your next speech goes well, you need to take action before your speech starts and introduce yourself to your room. This introduction can start long before the day of your speech thanks to today's new social media tools.

The details of how you give your speech have a big influence on how you speak. From what topic you pick, to your decision to either use or not use handouts, you are in control of how your audience experiences your next speech.

The most important thing that we need to do in order to become a better speaker is to make sure that every speech that we give has a clear point. This will happen when you know how to plan an effective speech.

This book will show you how to plan your speech in order to transform it into something that is even more powerful than it is today. We're going to show you how to find out what you should be doing and how to create a plan that will boost the impact of your speaking.

For more information on what it takes to be a great public speaker, check out my blog, The Accidental Communicator, at:

www.TheAccidentalCommunicator.com

Good luck!

- Dr. Jim Anderson

About The Author

I must confess that I never set out to be a public speaker. When I went to school, I studied Computer Science and thought that I'd get a nice job programming and that would be that. Well, at least part of that plan worked out!

My first job was working for Boeing on their F/A-18 fighter jet program. I spent my days programming fighter jet software in assembly language and I loved it. The U.S. government decided to save some money and went looking for other countries to sell this plane to. This put me into an unfamiliar role: I started to meet with foreign military officials and I ended up having to give speeches in order to explain what my product did.

Time moved on and so did I. I found myself working for Siemens, the big German telecommunications company. They were making phone switches and selling them to the seven U.S. phone companies. The problem was that the switches were too complicated. Customers couldn't tell the difference between one complicated phone switch from another complicated phone switch. Once again I found myself standing in front of the room giving speeches in order to explain what these complicated machines did and why ours were better than anyone else's.

I've spent over 25 years working as a product manager for both big companies and startups. This has given me an opportunity to do many, many presentations for customers, at conferences, and everywhere in-between.

I now live in Tampa Florida where I spend my time managing my consulting business, Blue Elephant Consulting, teaching college courses at the University of South Florida, and traveling to work with companies like yours to share the knowledge that I have about how to create and deliver powerful and effective speeches.

I'm always available to answer questions and I can be reached at:

Dr. Jim Anderson
Blue Elephant Consulting
Email: jim@BlueElephantConsulting.com
Facebook: http://goo.gl/1TVoK
Web: **www.BlueElephantConsulting.com**

"Unforgettable communication skills that will set your ideas free..."

<u>Create Speeches That Motivate Your Audiences And Get Your Message Heard!</u>

Dr. Jim Anderson is available to provide training and coaching on the topics that are the most important to people who have to speak in public: how can I create a speech that people want to hear and how can I deliver in a way that will allow me to connect with my audience and get my point across to them?

Dr. Anderson believes that in order to both learn and remember what he says, speakers need to laugh. Each one of his speeches is full of fun and humor so that what he says "sticks" with everyone.

Dr. Anderson's Public Speaking Training Includes:

1. How to plan your next speech: pick your purpose and understand your audience.
2. What's the best way to get PowerPoint and Keynote to work with you, not against you?
3. What do you need to do when you are presenting in order to truly connect with your audience?

Dr. Jim Anderson presents over 100 speeches per year. To invite Dr. Anderson to speak at your event, contact him at:

Phone: 813-418-6970 or
Email: jim@BlueElephantConsulting.com

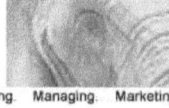

Blue Elephant Consulting has created the **Clear Blue™ Presentation System** for creating and delivering powerful and memorable presentations. The contents of this book are based on lessons learned during the development of the Clear Blue system. Contact Blue Elephant Consulting to learn more about the Clear Blue presentation system.

Chapter 1

Speaker: You Are What You Wear

Chapter 1: Speaker: You Are What You Wear!

The purpose of giving any speech is to be able to reach out and connect with your audience. No matter whether you are trying to inform them, entertain them, or convince them to take some action, none of this can be done unless you are able to make a connection with them. What you say is an important part of doing this, but did you know that **what you wear also plays a role**?

What Your Clothes Say about You

I'm hoping that most of us already know enough to "**dress up**" when we go to give a speech. If you pick up any popular book on public speaking, you'll find advice like "be the best dressed person in the room" and such.

What's interesting is that it's probably too much of a simplification to think of our clothes as being just that – clothes. Instead, Karen Hudson who retired from the movie business says that we should think about what we are wearing as being costumes that are "**scenery on the move**".

Now I can already see some of you starting to roll your eyes – I mean really, costumes? Give me just a minute to explain. Your time with your audience is **limited** - 15, 30, 60 minutes, right? You need to grab their attention, hold it, and make a difference in their lives.

What tools do you have to do this with? Sure your words are important. Probably how you say the words (pitch, tone, etc.) also plays a role. However, what else do you have? Not much! If you can start to think about what you are wearing as being yet another **speaking tool**, then all of a sudden you've got another "lever to pull" to get your audience to connect with you.

Different Speeches Require Different Types of Clothes

Not all speeches are the same. In fact, you need to be aware of what type of speech you will be giving and then you need to **dress appropriately** in order to lend even more power to your speech.

Speaking To Inform

When you are speaking to inform your audience you will be presenting either a lot of information or technical concepts in order to make your point. When doing this type of speaking, **first impressions** are quickly made by your audience when they are trying to determine if they are going to make the effort to listen to what you have to say.

For this type of speech your goal is going to be to **establish your credibility** in the field in which you are going to be talking about at first glance. You have two things that you want to quickly accomplish: you want your audience to understand that you are an expert in this field, and you want them to accept your credibility for speaking to them. What all this means is that your clothes have to convey a sense of strength, power, and leadership to your audience.

Speaking To Inspire

Things change when the purpose of your speech is to inspire your audience to **take some action**. What you are trying to do is to relate a story to your audience in a way that will provide them with a new point-of-view that will cause them to make a change.

For this type of speech, you are not trying to overpower your audience with your credibility. Instead, what you really want to do is to be able to inspire your audience. This means that you want your audience to reach out to you – to **accept your ideas as theirs** and to then grow because of these ideas.

This means that you want to come across as being three things all at once: credible, authoritative, and accessible. From a clothing point-of-view, this means that you are going to want to be **less formal** than you would be for a speech in which you were speaking to inform. Your clothing should present your audience with a softer, more conversational image of you.

Speaking To Entertain

Arguably you have the widest range of clothing choices when you are giving a speech that is designed to entertain your audience. Ultimately you are going to be telling your audience a story and you hope that by doing this you'll be able to **grab their attention** and hold on to it throughout your entire presentation. In the end your goal is to allow them to fully enjoy what you have to tell them.

Your clothing can be a key part of how you go about doing this. Depending on the story that you are going to be sharing with your audience, your clothing can **set the stage** before you even open your mouth. You can go all out and dress up in a full costume, or you can simply add a particular accessory to what you would normally wear (e.g. an Abraham Lincoln top hat) in order to make your audience eager to hear your story from the moment they first lay eyes on you.

Final Thoughts

Hudson points out that when she was taking a screenwriting class, she learned that each character must **contribute to the**

outcome of the story. You can say the same thing about the clothes that you wear to give a speech: each item must contribute directly to the telling of the story and its final outcome.

This leads to the **three key guidelines** that control what we wear when we are speaking:

1. The clothes should never take the focus off of you, the speaker.

2. No matter what you wear, you will need to be able to perform comfortably and effectively in the costume and accessories.

3. Time is of the essence – your costume should not tell more story than you have time to present.

Take the time to pick the clothes that you wear to match the speech that you will be giving and you'll be able to intimately connect with your audience and make a **lasting impact** in their lives.

Chapter 2

How to Rig a Speech to Get the Outcome You Want Every Time

Chapter 2: How to Rig a Speech to Get the Outcome You Want Every Time

You can't always do it all by yourself. If you want to make a lasting impression on your audience, then sometimes you just **got to bring in some help** to pull it off. Speakers who are ready to move up to the next level in their speaking often come to me and ask for advice. Now that they've gotten over their fear of speaking, they want to move on and start to make more of an impact with their audience. It's time to bring out an advanced speaking skill – rigging a speech.

The Setup

If as a speaker you can put aside your ego long enough to admit that sometimes if you really want to make a lasting impression on your audience, then you are going to have to allow others to help you, then you'll be **half-way there**.

An **advanced speaking technique** is to work with an outsider to act as a "**plant**" in the audience. Having somebody in the audience who you control gives you enormous power as a speaker when it comes to steering the audience's mood and reactions.

The most important part of stacking the deck is to make sure that you **take the time to rehearse** what you want to happen with your partner in crime – these things don't just happen by themselves.

The Action

When you rig a speech, you need to make sure that you've **carefully scripted** what you want to happen. The three most common uses of a plant are to generate anger, humor, and questions.

Having a member of your audience stand up and angrily shout something out or accuse you of something is a fantastic tool; however, it's just about as **dangerous as nitroglycerin**. This is an unexpected action – your audience will not be expecting it and so it will wake them up and grab their attention. I've used this one when I knew that what the audience would be thinking at a certain point was directly opposite to what I was telling them. Since you knew that it was coming, you have a fantastic response ready for them, this calms your angry audience member down, and everyone else is very impressed with you. That's exactly what I did and it took the tension out of the room.

Humor is difficult enough to try to do by yourself let alone with a partner, but if you can pull it off you'll be able to make a lasting impression on your audience. As with all types of humor, **timing is everything here**. One of my favorite techniques is to have my plant ask a question and then we end up getting involved in a very fast back-and-forth dialog that amazes and entertains everyone. Once upon a time I answered my plant's question by saying that something would take 1 year, they replied with 2, I said "3", they said "4" and so on.

Finally, one of the worst things that a speaker can do is to wrap up a speech by asking "**does anyone have any questions**" and then be greeted by dead silence. This is when having a plant can save your life: have them stand up and ask an interesting or controversial question just to get things going. Since you know what they are going to ask, you can structure your speech so that your answer to that question is really part of your speech.

What All of This Means for You

When you are ready to take your speaking skills up to the next level, starting to "**seed**" the audience with your trained agents is a great way to ensure that you are able to control how the speech will flow. These agents can control the audience's mood: get them angry, make them laugh, or ask the questions that they are all thinking about.

As with all tools, the planted agent **requires skill to use**. You have to take the time both to structure your speech in such a way as to accommodate your plant and to rehearse what each of you is going to say before the big day. Do it right and you'll have left your audience with a positive lasting impression.

Chapter 3

Business Speaking Is Unlike Any Other Speaking

Chapter 3: Business Speaking Is Unlike Any Other Speaking

Welcome to the world of business: do you know how to give a speech here? All too often speakers spend their time studying how to connect with customers and community members. That's all well and good; however, that **style of speaking** is completely different from the style that you need to use when you are giving a presentation within the company. Do you have the right stuff?

The Four Skills That You Need To Know

When you are giving a speech or presentation within your company, you need to take the time to **do it in a business-like manner** – there's a whole bunch of rules that you need to know about. A business audience has an expectation of how you are going to talk to them and what you're going to say. If you don't do this right, then they are going to tune you out very quickly.

There are **four specific skills** that you need to have mastered in order to make your next business presentation go well. Here they are:

- **Make Your Brain Big:** business is all about what is happening right now. This means that any time that you are giving a business presentation you need to make sure that your presentation is packed with current events. World events, industry changes, etc. are what your business audience wants to know about.

- **Practice Verbal Dancing:** Business speeches rarely go as you had planned them. What this means is that you've got to be ready for interruptions, questions, and redirection by senior management at any time during your speech. The key skill that you need to have is the ability to remain calm as your carefully planned speech does a 180-degree turn and heads off into a direction that you had never planned on going.

- **Become a Tailor:** In business, there is no such thing as a "canned speech". You may have a basic set of points that you want to communicate to several different audiences, but you'll need to change the words that you use and how you deliver the speech to meet the needs of each audience that you give it to.

- **Use the Power of Words:** Ultimately all we have to work with is words. A business audience is like any other audience and it's the words that you use that will determine if your speech ends up having any impact on them. Picking the right words to use for the right speech can make all of the difference in the world.

What All of This Means for You

There are many different types of speeches that we may be called on to give, but a business speech to the members of our own company can be **one of the toughest speeches to give**.

These types of speeches require **a special set of skills**. We need to take the time to make sure that our speech will meet the business need of our audience. Sorry, no generic speech will work here.

The real power comes from delivering this type of speech correctly. It's a skill that **too few speakers have**. If you can develop the skills that are needed to do this well, then you will have made yourself irreplaceable.

Chapter 4

Good Speakers Know How to Work a Room

Chapter 4: Good Speakers Know How to Work a Room

Speakers who **want to be successful** know that they have to connect with their audience. How to do this is the ultimate question that we've struggled with for years. I'm not claiming that I have all of the answers, but when I recently gave a keynote speech I had a chance to practice my "working the room" skills...

Arrive Early, Make Friends

Making a connection with your audience **starts with you taking the time to meet them**. In my case, I had been invited to deliver the keynote speech at Product Camp Chicago and the event was scheduled to start at 9:00 am.

I showed up at 8:30am – pretty much the same time as the folks who were setting up the event started to show up. This gave me a chance to meet the organizers before attendees started to show up and **things got really crazy**.

Since I was there I also had an opportunity to meet just about everyone who came when they arrived. This was no more than a handshake and a quick greeting. However, what it did was to transform me from "the keynote guy" into **somebody that they actually knew**.

Talk, Talk, Talk

Once everyone had arrived, **I really started to work the room**. You've probably heard this phrase before, but knowing what it means is the trick.

In my case, I took the time to move around the room where the audience was assembling. I'd approach a group of two or three attendees and start to chat with them. Instead of saying "hi, I'm the keynote speaker" (that's all about me), I'd say hi, ask for their names and ask them what they did for a living **(all about them).** Most of the time we'd end up talking about what they did and why they were there and who I was or what I was doing there often didn't come up.

Add Local Content to Your Speech

If you want to make the words that you say during your speech really connect with your audience, then you need to make sure that those words are words that **they can relate to**.

One of the simplest ways to make this happen is to **work local content into your speech**. I think that I can provide an example of this. During the discussions that I had with audience members before giving my keynote, I happened to discover that a number of them happened to be working in the casino gaming industry.

I was able to use this information to **add local content to my speech**. I worked a number of comments about "placing your bets" and "spinning the wheel" etc. into my speech. This was a wink and a nudge to the folks who were in the gaming industry and they all understood the references.

Leave Last, Make More Friends

All too often speakers think that **when they stop speaking, their job is over**. It turns out that this is not true. What folks don't realize is that your opportunities to connect with your audience continue long after the actual speech is done.

When my speech was done, I attended other speeches that went on that day, ate lunch with folks, and generally tried to make myself as available as possible. I met some great people and also **made myself more approachable** to just about everyone who was in the audience.

What All of This Means for You

The success of any speech that you give will be judged by the connection that you are able to make with your audience. The words that you use during your speech are important, **but they don't do the entire job**.

To make a good connection, **you need to make yourself available to your audience**. This means showing up early, chatting with your audience, working local content into your actual speech, and hanging out after your speech is done to further connect with your audience.

As speakers **it is how you are going to be remembered by each audience that really matters**. You control how this is all going to turn out. Take the time to really meet and interact with your audience and you'll be remembered in a positive way long after your speech is over and done with.

Chapter 5

Why Every Public Speaker Should Be "Tweeting"
(This Means You)

Chapter 5: Why Every Public Speaker Should Be "Tweeting" (This Means You)

Will these Internet crazes never end? Just in case you've been living under a rock someplace and haven't heard about the "Twitter" revolution, guess what: it's arrived and this time around as a public speaker you should be an active participant.

Just What Is This Twitter Thing?

If you're already "tweeting" every day, you can skip this part! In a nutshell, Twitter is sort of like the Citizen Band radios of the mid to late 1970s. Once you set up a Twitter account, you can either use the Twitter web page or download and install one of countless Twitter utilities to send out short messages telling the world what you are doing at any given point-in-time.

The key word here is "short" – a Twitter message (a "tweet" to those of us in the know), is limited to no more than 140 characters. Clearly we're not talking about sending out emails here.

Just to round out our comparison of Twitter to CBs, with a CB you needed to be on a certain radio channel if you wanted to hear what someone was saying. In the world of Twitter you need to be "following" someone if you want to be able to receive and read their tweets.

Why Should A Speaker Care About This Twitter Thing?

So outside of being the latest Internet craze, why should someone who is interested in becoming a better public speaker spend any time looking into this whole Twitter thing? It turns out that there are three reasons: practice, info, and followers.

One of the most important and challenging things that a speaker does is to write their speech. Although what you want to say may be clear in your head, actually getting the words on paper that will make it clear in your audience's heads is a completely different matter.

Twitter's limitation on how much information that you can pack into a single message, 140 characters, is both a curse and a blessing. It's a curse for those of us (me included) who are very verbose and who will use two words when one would do just fine.

It's a blessing in that if you want to clearly communicate an idea in just 140 characters then you're going to have to do a great deal of self-editing. You're going to end up throwing away all of that fancy prose that you use and boiling your tweets down to just the core essence of what you want to say.

This is exactly what you should be doing when you are writing a speech –get rid of the fluff and just leave the good stuff. By getting involved in the world of Twitter and actually spending time handcrafting your tweets, you'll refine your skills in this area. Sure, you could pay an expensive editor to help you refine your next speech, but it sure is cheaper to spend time on Twitter and learn to do it yourself.

Say Hello to Info

A nice side benefit to becoming active in the world of Twitter is that you'll grow a community of people who choose to follow you. This collection of people who may see every tweet that you send out are an incredibly valuable resource.

Pulling together a speech is not an easy thing to do. Finding the information that you need and running what you are going to say by interested people are critical things that you need to do.

Your Twitter followers are the perfect source for information and recommendations as well as being able to provide quick feedback on just about anything you want to run by them.

It's All About Followers

Finally, a speaker without an audience does nobody any good. Every time you open your mouth to give a speech, you'd really like there to not be an empty chair in the house.

The more followers that you have on Twitter, the better your ability to get the word out about your next speaking engagement. No, not every one of your followers will be able to attend your speech (it's a global service after all), but they sure will be able to pass the word on and you'd be amazed at how powerful a force this can be.

What All of This Means for You

It's starting to look as though the Internet tool called Twitter is here to stay. As more and more people sign up and start to "tweet", this is starting to become a genuine communication tool.

Speakers need to dive right in and start to use Twitter. The benefits are three-fold: using Twitter teaches speakers how to concisely express their thoughts, it provides a new way to gather information and test ideas, and finally it is a great way to advertise your next speech.

All new things can be a bit intimidating at first. CB radios had their own lingo and user community when they first appeared. Don't be nervous about using Twitter, get started and find out just how eloquent you can be in just 140 characters!

Chapter 6

The Ultimate Public Speaking Question: What to Speak About?

Chapter 6: The Ultimate Public Speaking Question: What to Speak About?

What's the first thing that runs through your head **when you are asked to give a speech?** If you are like most of us it's something along the lines of "what the heck am I going to speak about?" How to go about picking a speech topic that will keep your audience's attention and make them use their listening skills is the key to delivering a successful speech...

Things That Can Create Speeches

All too often when we have been asked to deliver a speech, we sit back and try to come up with something great to talk about. If we **overthink something like this** we run the risk of creating a speech that our audience won't be able to connect to while we give it. It would be like giving a bad speech using great presentation tips – in the end a bad speech design is going to result in our speech not being remembered.

Instead, we need to make sure that any speech that we create is **grounded in reality**. This is part of the importance of public speaking. We have to base it on something that our audience can relate to and that will allow them to connect with us. More often than not, the right place to start with creating your next speech is sitting right in front of you.

Take a look around you where you are sitting right now. No matter if you are at home, in the office, at school, or in a café somewhere, the surroundings should be familiar. What objects that exist in this environment **mean something to you?**

It's these objects that can serve as the foundation for your next speech. What is the object? Why does it mean something to you? What's its story? These are all very interesting pieces of information that can be worked into your next speech. Yes, you've been asked to give a speech for a specific reason. However, if you can use the objects from your surroundings to create a framework on which to build a speech, then you'll be able to **relate it back to your speech's topic**. In the end, your audience will enjoy your speech and they'll be able to connect with you.

Events That Can Create Speeches

Every audience wants to learn something from the next speech that they attend. What this means for you is that you're going to have to **share something with them** that they have not heard before. We've all had so many similar experiences that at times this can seem to be challenging.

However, as a speaker you need to realize that you have had experiences that **nobody else in your audience has had**. Or you've had the same experiences that they've had, but they turned out differently. What this means is that you've got stories to tell to your audience.

You don't have to have pulled people from a burning building or have climbed the world's tallest mountain. A lot of what your audience wants to hear you talk about can be considered to be somewhat mundane – they want to know how you've **met regular everyday challenges** and how you've been successful.

The next time that you are asked to give a speech, consider what you are being asked to speak about and then give some thought to **the events and experiences that you've had**. Do you have something that you can use to build an experience-based framework on for giving your next speech?

What All of This Means for You

We are all living busy, complicated lives and it turns out that this is great news. The next time that we're asked to give a speech, it's **the chaos of our lives** that we can draw from to create a great speech – this is one of the benefits of public speaking.

One great source of speech topics is to look around ourselves and identify **all of the objects that are in our lives**. Although some of these objects may be mundane, how they came into our lives or what they mean to us can serve as the basis of a speech.

Another source of possible speech topics are **the events that are occurring or which have occurred in our lives**. These events are unique to us – nobody else has experienced anything exactly like them. This is where the power of our ability to tell a story about one or more of these events can serve as the foundation of our next speech.

As speakers we have an obligation to our next audience to **deliver a great speech**. In order to make this happen, we need to be able to build a speech that will be memorable to them. If we'll take the time to look around us at the objects and the events that are in our lives, we'll be able to create memorable speeches that will make an impact in the lives of our audiences.

Chapter 7

Public Speakers Want to Know: Are Handouts Your Friend or Foe?

Chapter 7: Public Speakers Want to Know: Are Handouts Your Friend or Foe?

How much information is there going to be in your next speech? Most of the speeches that we give are full of great information that our audiences would like to **remember and follow-up on** — your audience understands the importance of public speaking and that's why they are there. That's where the problem shows up: when a speaker provides his or her audience with a handout there's a good chance that you are going to lose their attention. What's a speaker to do?

One at a Time

Although the handout that you've created for your audience may be full of great information, you are facing **a serious problem** when you get ready to hand it out to your audience: should you give it to them before you speak or after you speak?

If you give your handout to your audience before you deliver your speech, **they may spend their time reading your handout and not paying attention to you**. Additionally, if like most of us you just print out the slides that you will be presenting and give it to your audience as a handout, then they'll always be two slides ahead of you and still won't be paying attention to what you are saying right now.

If you decide to avoid this situation and distribute your handout after you are all done giving your speech, then do you really think that anyone is ever going to **take the time to look at them?** For that matter, where did your audience write down the notes that they took during your speech – was the information that they were trying to remember available in your handouts?

One way to deal with this problem is to use a combination approach: provide your handouts to your audience as you reach that point in your presentation. Clearly this takes some effort and the rustle of papers being handed out over and over will tend to take away from your speech. However, **the benefits can be enormous**.

Since each handout will show up just when you start to talk about what's on it, your audience will have no problems making their notes on the correct handout. Limiting the handouts that they have to material that you've either already talked about or are just getting ready to cover **prevents them from jumping ahead of you**.

Fill In the Blank

Another way of making it so that you can use handouts with your next presentation without taking away from what you are saying is to **use the fill-in-the-blank technique**. This approach is a less disruptive than the one-at-a-time technique.

When you use the fill-in-the-blank technique your audience will be handed a complete set of your handouts before you start to speak. However, the handouts that they receive will be incomplete – **information will be missing**.

During your presentation you will show slides and you will discuss issues that contain the information that is missing from your audience's slides. As you do this, they can write down what you've just said and when your speech is over, **their handouts will be full of valuable information**.

This approach allows you to strike a balance between making sure that your audience has the information that they'll need in order to remember what you said while not allowing your handouts to **distract from the speech that you are giving**. No solution is perfect, but this technique seems to do a good job.

What All of This Means for You

The benefits of public speaking include **sharing the information that we have with our audience**. Sometimes we have so much information that some form of a handout is called for in order to help our audience to remember everything that we've told them.

The problem with handouts is that they can **distract our audience from paying attention to what we are saying**. There are several different ways to deal with this problem. The first is to hand out the different pages in the handout as you reach that point in your speech. Another approach is to remove important information from each slide and force your audience to pay attention in order to fill out the handouts.

Handouts are becoming a more and more critical part of every speech that we give as we **load our speeches up with additional information**. Give some thought to how you want to share your information with your audience while keeping their attention throughout your speech.

Chapter 8

Business Speaking: What to Do, What Not to Do

Chapter 8: Business Speaking: What to Do, What Not to Do

Giving a speech in a business environment, specifically **to a group of senior managers**, can be one of the most difficult speeches that any of us will ever be called on to give. However, even this type of speech can be done smoothly and will allow you to be seen as an effective communicator if only you take the time to follow the following suggestions.

What You Need To Do During a Business Speech

I'd like to be able to tell you that there is just one set of presentation tips that we all need to know in order to make sure that our next speech to the people who are running the company will not only hear what we have to say, but also take action based on it. The reality is that there are **a number of different things** that you're going to have to do all at the same time in order to realize the importance of public speaking in this type of business environment.

The first of these is to make sure that you set aside enough time to practice the speech that you've written. The reason that you're going to want to do this is because when you actually deliver your speech, you are going to want to **make it sound natural** – that is, not like you are giving a speech. Although you don't want to come across as being too informal, you also want to connect with your audience and by taking the time to practice your speech the words will flow out of you naturally.

The next thing that you are going to want to do is to take the mystery out of why you are giving the speech. You've been invited to present to your senior management and it turns out that generally they have fairly poor listening skills. What this means is that they can either leave or cut you off at any time if they don't understand why you are wasting their time. In order to prevent this from happening, you need to **clearly state what your speech is all about** right off the bat. With a little luck, this will capture everyone's attention and you can then move on to providing them with more details and background information.

Finally, you need to take the time to **paint a mental picture** of what the future could look like. If you want your senior management to agree with the ideas that you are presenting in your speech, then you are going to have to use your speech to paint a vivid mental image in their heads of what the future could look like if they approve what you are proposing.

What You Need To Not Do During a Business Speech

Just as important as doing the right things during a speech is, making sure that you **don't do the wrong things** is just as important in order to achieve the benefits of public speaking. It would be a shame if you did everything correctly, and then ended up still not having your ideas accepted by your senior management. Here's one thing that you need to make sure your speech does not contain.

Just about the worst thing that you can do when you are giving a business presentation is to try to make it appear perfect **by memorizing it**. If you write out every word that you are going to say and then you memorize it that way, you are going to come across as being stiff and brittle. The smallest distraction during your speech may cause you to lose your place and the whole thing will come crashing down on you.

Instead, do take the time to memorize the opening and the closing of your speech. How you word both of these parts of your speech is very important so memorizing them makes a lot of sense. Use **bullet points** to keep track of the middle of your speech and that will allow you to cover the important stuff while still sounding natural to your audience.

What All of This Means for You

Making a business presentation to a group of senior managers can be both a nerve racking and **a career limiting event**. You can do this successfully; however, in order to be successful you need to do the right things and not do the wrong things.

The **right things** consist of taking the time to practice your speech before you give it, opening your speech by telling your audience what your main point is, and painting a picture of what the future could look like if the senior managers adopt your speech's proposal.

The ultimate goal of any speech that we give is to **change the world** in some way. Giving a business presentation to senior management allows us to make this happen if we take the time to do it correctly

Chapter 9

Break Glass In Case of Speech

Chapter 9: Break Glass In Case Of Speech

In a perfect world, we would always be given plenty of time to prepare for our next speech. However, you and I don't live in a perfect world and that means that because of the importance of public speaking all too often the opportunity to give a speech **will just suddenly show up**. My question for you is simple: will you be ready?

Know Your Topic

Since you can never be sure when you'll be called on to give a speech, or for that matter who your audience will be, you need to make sure that **you control the things that you can control**. This means that you need to pick a topic that appeals to you.

When you give **your back-pocket speech**, it's going to be important that your audience realizes that you really care about your topic. By picking a topic that you both know and care about, it will be easy for your passion to come out.

Take Time to Prepare

This may be the hardest thing to do: prepare to give a speech that nobody has asked you to give for an audience that you don't know anything about. Yes, I know that this sounds sort of crazy, but you need to practice this speech every so often in order to **keep it fresh in your mind**.

The one thing that you do need to be careful of is to **not over practice your speech**. This means that you don't want to practice it so much that when you deliver it you'll just slide in to an automatic mode. Your audience will realize that you are on autopilot and they'll tune you out.

Find Out How to Relax

The last tip for how to be ready to give a back-pocket speech is the hardest to do: **learn how to relax**. If you have plenty of time to prepare for a speech, generally speaking, your level of confidence will grow as you have time to get comfortable with the event, the speech, and your audience. When called on to give a back-pocket speech you won't have any of these.

What this means is that you are going to have to be able to rely on the prep work that you've already done in order to **quickly calm yourself down**. Knowing that you are ready to give the speech at any time will go a long way to helping you keep your nerves under control. Take the time to create a great speech and to practice it and you'll be ready when the time finally comes to give it.

What All of This Means for You

You really don't have any control over when your next speaking opportunity is going to show up. What this means that that you need to **always have a back-pocket speech ready to go** so that when called upon, you can step up and deliver a memorable speech – knowing that you have to be ready to do this is one of the benefits of public speaking.

In order to have a speech that will be ready to go when you need it, you must first **pick a topic to talk on**, and then practice it. Finally, you need to take the time to teach yourself how to relax.

Although you can't be sure when you'll be asked to give a speech, you can be assured that **you will be asked**. What this means is that you need to always be ready. It turns out that it's not all that hard to do, just take the time to prepare and you'll be ready when your name gets called!

Chapter 10

How Speakers Should Handle Handouts

Chapter 10: How Speakers Should Handle Handouts

As a speaker the one thing that we want to accomplish during every speech that we give is to **make an impression on our audience**. We'd like to be able to convince them of the importance of public speaking and share with them some ideas that they can take with them and use even after our speech is over and done with. In order to make this happen we sometimes provide our audience with a handout. This is where things can start to get very confusing very quickly...

Are Handouts Good or Bad?

Among speakers there are **differing opinions** regarding handouts. The biggest problem seems to be the fact that if you hand your audience something to look at besides looking at you, they just might spend the rest of your speech reading the handout and not listening to you!

There are speakers who simply take the PowerPoint or Keynote slides that they are presenting, print them out, and then hand them out to their audience before their speech. I think that this is a bad idea – why should I listen to you if I have a copy of everything that you are going to be telling me. Yes, you might add some detail, but probably not enough to really matter – I can now **skip your speech** and go do something else without having to worry about missing anything important.

What we all need to keep in mind for any presentation is that **the most powerful visual aid** that we have available is ourselves. This means that the one thing that we don't want to have happen is to provide our audience with an opportunity to keep their heads down during our speech. There is a good chance that given the opportunity, the audience will be racing ahead of us a couple of slides in the handout no matter how fast we talk!

How Best To Hand Out Handouts

Ok, so if just giving your audience a copy of all of your slides is the wrong thing to do, what is the right thing to do? How about going through the deck of slides that you'll be presenting and **finding the ones that have the most information on them**. These are often flow charts or checklists. Print out the 4 or 5 slides that will provide real value to your audience and make these the handouts that are given to the audience.

Instead of handing your audience the entire set of handouts before you start to speak, enlist a helper and when you get to a point in your speech where a handout will be helpful, **have your assistant distribute it then**. This way you'll prevent your audience from spending their time reading ahead.

Finally, the one thing that you don't want have happen is for your handouts to give away all of your secrets. Instead, remove valuable information from your handouts and **leave blank spaces there**. Then when you are speaking, provide the information that goes into those spaces. Your audience will pay attention to you and then they'll write it down in order to capture your words. What a great way to learn!

What All of This Means for You

As speakers **we want to change the world with every speech that we give** — this is one of the benefits of public speaking. In order to make this happen, we need to provide our audiences with information that they can remember and start to use. Providing them with a handout might do the trick, but it comes with its own set of hazards.

One of the problems with handouts is that it can cause your audience to spend time reading the handouts and **not paying attention to your speech**. You can solve this by limiting the number of handouts that you provide and leaving important information off of them so that they will have to listen to you to get what they need.

I believe that a handout is a great idea. This way your audience doesn't have to be scrambling for a scrap of paper to write your best ideas down on. However, you need to think about how your handouts are going to be used and make sure that they are a tool that will help you in your goal of **keeping your audience's attention for your entire speech**.

Chapter 11

Hey Speaker – What's Your Point?

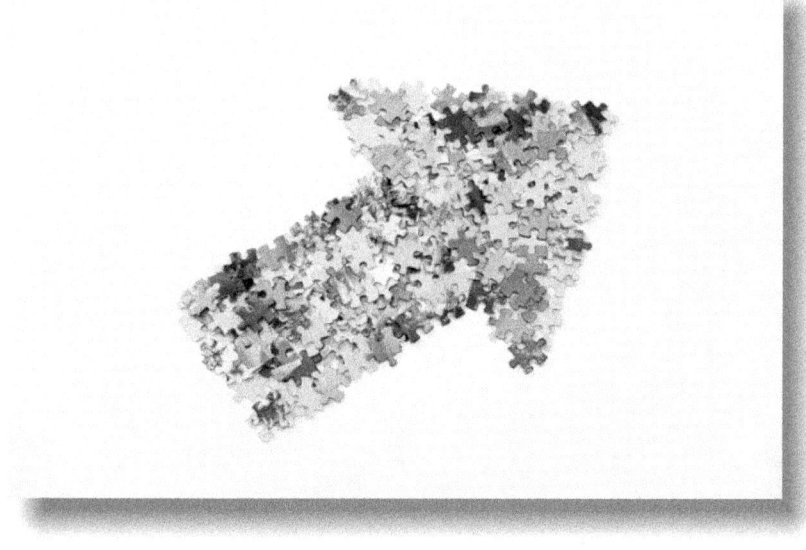

Chapter 11: Hey Speaker – What's Your Point?

What's the worst thing that speaker can do when delivering a speech? **Not get to the point!** Your audience is left wondering just exactly why they were willing to sit there though your speech when it seems as though there was no real reason for you to give the speech. What this means is that we've got to sharpen up our speaking abilities and get to the point!

Why Getting to the Point Matters

In the world of public speaking we spend a lot of time talking about how to start a speech in a way that will grab our audience's attention. This is a key point whenever we're talking about the importance of public speaking. However, perhaps we really should be spending our time talking about **what the best way to wrap up a speech is**. It turns out that the last words out of our mouths are the ones that our audiences are most likely to remember. Sure seems like this is where we should be spending a lot of our planning time.

The conclusion of your speech is where you get to make your main point. It's where you wrap up your speech and, just like in any good mystery novel; you get to reveal "who did it". The beauty of a well done conclusion is that it provides you with one more opportunity to **revisit what you've said and restate your main points**. This is your final opportunity to make sure that your audience will both understand and "get" your main point.

How to Make Sure That You Get To the Point

There is no way that you'll be able to share your main point with your audience if you never get to it. What this means for you is that you have a responsibility when you are designing your next speech to take the time and **plan out how you want to work your main point in**. If you make room for it, then you'll be sure to cover it during your speech.

The first thing that you are going to have to do is to **make time** to cover your main point. There are a number of different ways of going about doing this; however, my favorite is the 15-70-15 rule. This is where 15% of your time is spent on the opening, 70% is spent making your case during the middle, and then you spent the last 15% of your speech making your point during your conclusion.

The words that you use when you are making your point are critical. What this means is that you don't want to leave them to chance. Instead, take the time to write them out before you give your speech. This is the one time that **memorizing the words** that you are going to want to say is highly recommended.

What All of This Means for You

As speakers we have **an unwritten agreement with our audience**. They agree to sit through our speech and we agree to make sure that our speech has a point to it. This is one of the unstated benefits of public speaking. If we don't deliver, then our audience is going to quickly realize it and they are not going to be happy with us!

The reason that making sure that your speech has a point is so important is because **it's what closes your presentation –** everyone will realize that you are done. Your point is the thing that you want your audience to remember about your speech. That's why you have to plan your time wisely in order to ensure that you'll have enough time to make your point. Make sure that how you state your point is clearly done.

As speakers we give speeches because we want to make an impact on our audiences. In order for this to occur, we need to **make sure that they understand why we gave the speech in the first place**. Making sure that your next speech has a definite point is a critical part of doing this.

Chapter 12

Ways to Plan an Effective Speech

Chapter 12: Ways to Plan an Effective Speech

We all share the same goal: **we'd like to be able to deliver a great speech**. However, in order to do that, a number of different things have to come together at the same time for us. These include such things as having a good speech, having a receptive audience, and just a little bit of luck. I can't do anything about that luck thing, but I think that I've got a few suggestions that will help with everything else.

4 Tips for Creating an Effective Speech

Yes, we'd all like to be able to sit down and just let an effective speech flow out of us. However, all too often it doesn't seem to happen that way – what we end up with is a jumbled mess of thoughts. In order to demonstrate the importance of public speaking and create a speech that will both connect with our audience and show them that we've planned out what we wanted to share with them, **we need to follow the following four steps** when we are creating an effective speech:

- **Pick Your Purpose:** You have agreed to give a speech: why? What is the purpose of you writing a speech, practicing it, getting all dressed up, and being willing to deal with the nerves associated with standing in front of a group of strangers? Is your purpose the right one to share with this audience and are you the right person to be doing it? Finally, do you really care about this purpose – if you don't then you shouldn't be up there.

- **Know Your Audience:** If you want your next speech to be effective, then you are going to have to have a good understanding of who you'll be talking to. How big will your audience be? Who is going to be in your audience (age, gender, profession, political views, etc)? Why are they there to listen to you?

- **Clearly State Your Main Point:** The reason that you are giving this speech needs to be something that you can sum up in a single sentence. Make sure that you know what this sentence is. Once you have identified this point, make sure that you have at least three supporting points that all serve to bolster your main point. Pull all of this together, and you'll have yourself an effective speech.

- **Back It Up:** If you want to use your effective speech to win your audience over to your way of thinking, then you're going to have to present them with the evidence that you are right. Make sure that you've taken the time to do your homework and you've got a compelling set of evidence that will support your viewpoint including: fact & figures, stories, definitions, examples, etc.

What All of This Means for You

The success of your next speech may be determined before you even take the stage. If you've done all of the planning that is necessary, then the benefits of public speaking will be yours and **you've set yourself up for success**.

In order to plan your next speech you are going to have to take the time to **define your purpose** and make sure that you know who is going to be in your audience. Every speech has a central point – make sure that you know what yours is. Finally, make sure that you have the evidence that you're going to need in order to back up the point that you are making.

The good news is that you can deliver powerful and effective speeches. What you need to do is to make sure that the take the time before your speech to **plan out what you want to say**

and how you want to say it. Do your homework and I'm sure that you'll be pleased with the results!

It's from the forge of failure that the steel of success is formed.

Hard Work Does Not Guarantee Success, But Success Does Not Happen Without Hard Work.

— Dr. Jim Anderson

Create Speeches That Motivate Your Audiences And Get Your Message Heard!

Dr. Jim Anderson is available to provide training and coaching on the topics that are the most important to people who have to speak in public: how can I create a speech that people want to hear and how can I deliver in a way that will allow me to connect with my audience and get my point across to them?

Dr. Anderson believes that in order to both learn and remember what he says, speakers need to laugh. Each one of his speeches is full of fun and humor so that what he says "sticks" with everyone.

Dr. Anderson's Public Speaking Training Includes:

1. How to plan your next speech: pick your purpose and understand your audience.
2. What's the best way to get PowerPoint and Keynote to work with you, not against you?
3. What do you need to do when you are presenting in order to truly connect with your audience?

Dr. Jim Anderson presents over 100 speeches per year. To invite Dr. Anderson to speak at your event, contact him at: **Phone: 813-418-6970** or **Email:** jim@BlueElephantConsulting.com

Photo Credits:

Cover - By: Teresa Robinson
https://www.flickr.com/photos/stargardener/

Chapter 1 – By: On Aura Tout Vu
https://www.flickr.com/photos/oatvparis/

Chapter 2 – By: James Duncan Davidson
https://www.flickr.com/photos/oreilly/

Chapter 3 – By: Jonas K.
https://www.flickr.com/photos/jonask/

Chapter 4 – By: Wirawat Lian-udom
https://www.flickr.com/photos/mytudut/

Chapter 5 – By: Slava Murava Kiss
https://www.flickr.com/photos/woofer_kyyiv/

Chapter 6 – By: Rusty Sheriff
https://www.flickr.com/photos/rustysheriff/

Chapter 7 – By: Jessamyn West
https://www.flickr.com/photos/iamthebestartist/

Chapter 8 – By: Opensource.com
https://www.flickr.com/photos/opensourceway/

Chapter 9 – By: Jim Nix
https://www.flickr.com/photos/jimnix/

Chapter 10 – By: Joel Penner
https://www.flickr.com/photos/featheredtar/

Chapter 11 – By: Horia Varlan
https://www.flickr.com/photos/horiavarlan/

Chapter 12 – By: Johannes Lundberg
https://www.flickr.com/photos/johanneslundberg/

Other Books By The Author

Product Management

- How Product Managers Can Grow Their Career: How Product Managers Can Find And Succeed In The Right Job

- Product Management Secrets: Techniques For Product Managers To Boost Product Sales And Increase Customer Satisfaction

- Product Development Lessons For Product Managers: How Product Managers Can Create Successful Products

- Customer Lessons For Product Managers: Techniques For Product Managers To Better Understand What Their Customers Really Want

- Product Failure Lessons For Product Managers: Examples Of Products That Have Failed For Product Managers To Learn From

- Communication Skills For Product Managers: The Communication Skills That Product Managers Need To Know How To Use In Order To Have A Successful

Product

- How To Have A Successful Product Manager Career: The Things That You Need To Be Doing TODAY In Order To Have A Successful Product Manager Career

- Product Manager Product Success: How to keep your product on track and make it become a success

Public Speaking

- How To Become A Better Speaker By Changing How You Speak: Change techniques that will transform a speech into a memorable event

- How To Give A Great Presentation: Presentation techniques that will transform a speech into a memorable event

- How To Rehearse In Order To Give The Perfect Speech: How to effectively rehearse your next speech to that your message be remembered forever!

- Secrets To Creating The Perfect Speech: How to create a speech that will make your message be remembered forever!

- Secrets To Organizing The Perfect Speech: How to organize the best speech of your life!

- Secrets To Planning The Perfect Speech: How to plan to give the best speech of your life

- How To Show What You Mean During A Presentation: How to use visual techniques to transform a speech into a memorable event

CIO Skills

- What CIOs Need To Know About Working With Partners: Techniques For CIOs To Use In Order To Be Able To Successfully Work With Partners

- Critical CIO Management Skills: Decision Making Skills That Every CIO Needs To Have In Order To Be Able To Make The Right Choices

- How CIOs Can Make Innovation Happen: Tips And Techniques For CIOs To Use In Order To Make Innovation Happen In Their IT Department

- CIO Communication Skills Secrets: Tips And Techniques For CIOs To Use In Order To Become

Better Communicators

- Managing Your CIO Career: Steps That CIOs Have To Take In Order To Have A Long And Successful Career

- CIO Business Skills: How CIOs can work effectively with the rest of the company!

IT Manager Skills

- How IT Managers Can Make Innovation Happen: Tips And Techniques For IT Managers To Use In Order To Make Innovation Happen In Their Teams

- Staffing Skills IT Managers Must Have: Tips And Techniques That IT Managers Can Use In Order To Correctly Staff Their Teams

- Secrets Of Effective Leadership For IT Managers: Tips And Techniques That IT Managers Can Use In Order To Develop Leadership Skills

- IT Manager Career Secrets: Tips And Techniques That IT Managers Can Use In Order To Have A Successful Career

- IT Manager Budgeting Skills: How IT Managers Can Request, Manage, Use, And Track Their Funding

Negotiating

- Learn How To Signal In Your Next Negotiation: How To Develop The Skill Of Effective Signaling In A Negotiation In Order To Get The Best Possible Outcome

- Learn The Skill Of Exploring In A Negotiation: How To Develop The Skill Of Exploring What Is Possible In A Negotiation In Order To Reach The Best Possible Deal

- Learn How To Argue In Your Next Negotiation: How To Develop The Skill Of Effective Arguing In A Negotiation In Order To Get The Best Possible Outcome

- How To Open Your Next Negotiation: How To Start A Negotiation In Order To Get The Best Possible Outcome

- Preparing For Your Next Negotiation: What You Need To Do BEFORE A Negotiation Starts In Order To Get The Best Possible Deal

Miscellaneous

- The Internet-Enabled Successful School District Superintendent: How To Use The Internet To Boost Parental Involvement In Your Schools

- Power Distribution Unit (PDU) Secrets: What Everyone Who Works In A Data Center Needs To Know!

- Making The Jump: How To Land Your Dream Job When You Get Out Of College!

"How to plan a speech in order to achieve your goals and delight your audience"

> This book has been written with one goal in mind – to show you how you can plan a powerful and effective speech We're going to show you how to make sure that your next speech is a great speech!
>
> **Let's Make Your Next Speech A Success!**

What You'll Find Inside:

- **HOW TO RIG A SPEECH TO GET THE OUTCOME YOU WANT EVERY TIME**

- **PUBLIC SPEAKERS WANT TO KNOW: ARE HANDOUTS YOUR FRIEND OR FOE?**

- **WAYS TO PLAN AN EFFECTIVE SPEECH**

- **SPEAKER: YOU ARE WHAT YOU WEAR**

Dr. Jim Anderson brings his 25 years of real-world experience to this book. He's delivered speeches at some of the world's largest firms as well as at many conferences. He's going to show you what you need to do in order to make your next speech a success!

www.ingramcontent.com/pod-product-compliance
Lightning Source LLC
Chambersburg PA
CBHW071803170526
45167CB00003B/1152